3/4/08

PIZZA, PIGS, and Poetry

JACK PRELUTSKY

How
to write
a poem

 GREENWILLOW BOOKS
An Imprint of HarperCollinsPublishers

Collins is an imprint of HarperCollins Publishers.

Pizza, Pigs, and Poetry: How to Write a Poem
Copyright © 2008 by Jack Prelutsky

The text of this book is set in Zapf Ellip
Book design by Sylvie Le Floc'h

Library of Congress Cataloging-in-Publication Data

Prelutsky, Jack.
Pizza, pigs, and poetry : how to write a poem /
by Jack Prelutsky.
p. cm.
"Greenwillow Books."
ISBN 978-0-06-143449-5 — ISBN 978-0-06-143448-8 (pbk.)
1. Prelutsky, Jack—Juvenile literature.
2. Poetry—Authorship—Juvenile literature. I. Title.
PS3566.R36Z46 2008
811'.54—dc22
2007036738

First Edition 10 9 8 7 6 5 4 3 2 1

Greenwillow Books

For Virginia Duncan,
my wonderful editor

contents

PIZZA, PIGS, and Poetry

Hello!

I've been writing poetry for children for more than forty years and have had a wonderful time doing it. Over all those years I've learned quite a few things about writing poetry. Nobody ever told me about them, and I had to teach them to myself. It's also possible that I've invented some of them. I wish that I had known some of these techniques earlier. It would have made writing my poems a lot easier.

I've talked to thousands and thousands of

kids about writing poetry, and many of them have asked me questions about it. The most asked question has been "Where do you get your ideas?" I've explained that I get ideas by keeping my eyes and ears open and by paying attention to what's going on around me. I've also explained that *everyone* gets ideas—the trick is to know what to do with them.

One of most important things I do is to write down my ideas *immediately* in my notebook or at least on a scrap of paper. Otherwise, I'm certain to forget those ideas, and so there'll be poems that never happen. I talk about writing down your ideas and carrying a notebook several times in this book.

I use many techniques for writing poems and thought that it would be helpful to share the creative process with you. That's what this book is all about. Don't ask me about dactyls, quatrains, or iambic pentameter. There are many fine books that describe poetic forms, meters, and structures. In this book I'm letting you peek into my mind and see how I use my imagination to turn ideas into poems.

I hope that you enjoy reading *Pizza, Pigs, and Poetry* and that it inspires you to write your own poems.

Your friend,

Jack Prelutsky

My Father's Underwear

I'm going to admit something to you. When I was a little boy, a looooooong time ago, I was not the best-behaved little boy in the history of the United States of America. It's true! Every once in a while . . . actually pretty often . . . okay, every day, I did something that made my father mad at me.

My father was a wonderful man, but he was only human and did have his limits, so he got mad at me, and I'm sure I deserved it. When my father got mad at me, he did not run around and jump up and down and get all bent out of shape and yell and scream and cry and tear out his hair (he couldn't do that anyhow, because he was bald) and get hysterical and throw a tantrum. No . . . that was my mother's job.

My father was just the opposite. He suddenly got very quiet. His eyes narrowed, and his face grew serious, with the Western gunfighter look that says, "You got till sundown to ride on out of town or I'm a-comin' for you." His voice got very soft and very deep, and he simply gestured to me with his index finger and said, "Come here, son." Uh-oh! I knew that when my father said "Come here, son" in that certain special way, I was in big trouble.

You may wonder what I did in that situation. I did exactly the same thing that most of you would do. I denied everything. "No, no, Daddy!" I said. "I didn't do it. I'm innocent. I've been behaving. I've been a *good* boy . . . but I know who did it. My brother. He's right over there. Get him!" Amazingly, sometimes that worked. Sometimes it was even true. But of course my brother did the same thing to me, so it kind of evened out. Sometimes I got punished for things he did, sometimes he got punished for things I did, sometimes we both got punished even though we didn't do anything, and sometimes we didn't get punished at all when we deserved it. It all evened out.

One of the things that I did to make my father so mad at me was to pin his underwear up on the wall. Before I did that, though, I decorated it. You see, my father wore really boring white underwear, and I wanted to make it pretty, so I painted it with finger paint. *Then* I pinned it to the wall. My father didn't like that at all.

Once I put a bug in his coffee cup, and another time I put breadcrumbs in his bed. I did lots of other stuff too. I made a list of all the things like that I could remember, then picked some of them to put in a poem called "I Wonder Why Dad Is So Thoroughly Mad."

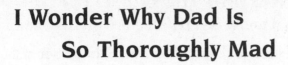

I Wonder Why Dad Is
So Thoroughly Mad

I wonder why Dad is so thoroughly mad,
I can't understand it at all,
unless it's the bee still afloat in his tea,
or his underwear, pinned to the wall.

Perhaps it's the dye on his favorite tie,
or the mousetrap that snapped in his shoe,
or the pipeful of gum that he found with
     his thumb,
or the toilet, sealed tightly with glue.

It can't be the bread crumbled up in his bed,
or the slugs someone left in the hall,
I wonder why Dad is so thoroughly mad,
I can't understand it at all.

℮ WRITING TIP #1 ℮ ℮ ℮ ℮ ℮ ℮

Unless you're a perfect child, and I doubt that you are—for I've met tens of thousands of children, and I've never met a perfect child yet—I suspect that you misbehave from time to time. Perhaps you're the way I was when I was a kid and like to play practical jokes on your parents or on your brothers and sisters. I pulled lots of practical jokes on my brother. The advantage of playing practical jokes on my brother rather than my parents was that he couldn't punish me for them.

Think about something you did, accidentally or on purpose, that made your parents mad at you. Write down as much about it as you can. Did you fling spaghetti at the ceiling? Did you draw on the wall with crayons? Did you switch the salt and the sugar? These are all wonderful things to write about. Write about how you did it, why you did it, and what happened when you did it. You'll have lots of fun writing about your own misbehavior. By the way, I did all those things . . . and more. You see, I also was not a perfect child, but you already knew that.

My Mother's Rules

My mother was just as wonderful as my father, but she drove me crazy. Sometimes I think that mothers exist mostly to drive their kids crazy. Of course kids absolutely exist to drive their mothers crazy. It's been going on like that for thousands of years, and there's no end in sight.

One of the things that my mother did to drive me crazy was make up rules. She had so many rules, and most of them started with the same word: *Don't.* "Don't do this, and don't do that, and don't do this, and don't do that, and don't do this . . . and don't *ever* do *that!*"

She had a special kind of rule that I'd like to tell you about, but first I have to give you a little more background. You see, when I was a kid, I discovered something that I strongly suspect you have also discovered for yourselves. I discovered that food was not only for eating. That's right, I figured out that I could do *other things* with food.

Now, that all probably started when I was just a little baby in the high chair, and my mother was trying to cram some horrible stuff into my face. You know what I'm talking about: mashed turnips and smashed carrots and destroyed broccoli. Well, I didn't want any of that stuff, so I flung it right back at her.

She used to try to give me medicine–
horrible, smelly, sticky red stuff in a spoon.
Of course I didn't want it, so I did my best to
avoid it. "Open wide!" she said. I just shook
my head and kept my lips closed tight. "Open
wide!" she said a little louder. I closed my
lips even tighter and shook my head even
more. "Open wide!" she said even louder. I
shook my head so hard that she might have
thought it would fly right off my neck. Then
she got mad. *"Open wide!"* she yelled just
about as loud as she could. I got scared and
opened my mouth. She stuck the spoon in,
and I closed my mouth. The medicine tasted
terrible, so instead of swallowing it, I opened
my lips just a little and sprayed her with it.

I used to do great stuff with food. One of

my favorites was mashed potatoes. There are lots of things you can do with mashed potatoes. Sometimes I'd make a big mound of them and then chop up the mound with the side of my hand. I also made mashed-potato snowmen on my plate, using peas for eyes, a carrot wedge for a nose, and a green bean for a mouth. Once I made a well in the middle of the mashed potatoes and filled it with gravy. Then I made a diving board out of Popsicle sticks and put a bug on it. Eventually the bug dropped into the gravy and sort of swam around. It was lots of fun to watch.

This reminds me of my "spaghetti bug." One day I smooshed a long strand of spaghetti onto the back of a cockroach and let it go. I'm sure that the cockroach wasn't happy about dragging that spaghetti around. Perhaps it was confused. In any event, it headed as quickly as it could for the safest, darkest place it could find, which in our kitchen was under the refrigerator. The cockroach had just made it to the refrigerator when my mother entered the kitchen. She saw that strand of spaghetti apparently moving by itself across the floor and let out a shriek.

I used to squeeze food. Different foods behave in different ways when you squeeze them; it really depends on what you're squeezing. If you squeeze a whole watermelon, nothing much happens. If you squeeze peas, they practically disappear. If you squeeze a tomato, it explodes, and if you squeeze an egg . . . well, that's just gross. Another food that's fun to squeeze takes practice and the right amount of mustard. Did you know that if you squeeze a hot dog just right, it'll shoot across the room?

My all-time favorite foods to play with may have been meatballs and spaghetti. They were fun together, and they were fun separately. I've already mentioned one thing that I did with a strand of spaghetti, but there were other things. I used to wear spaghetti. I made headbands, neckties, and belts out of spaghetti. I used spaghetti as a whip to try to zap flies and mosquitoes. I also used to shove spaghetti down my little brother's pants.

Did you know that I invented the meatball-and-spaghetti yo-yo? Well, I did. I'd stand at one end of the kitchen and wrap a long strand of spaghetti around a big meatball, then hold on to the spaghetti while I tossed the meatball underhand. I watched with tremendous pleasure as the spaghetti unwound and the meatball rolled across the floor to the other end of the kitchen. I do admit that it was a one-way yo-yo; the meatball didn't come back. So I had two choices: I could retrieve the meatball and rewind the spaghetti around it and send it back in the other direction, or I could get another meatball. I did both. I yo-yoed half a dozen or so meatballs across the kitchen floor, then gathered them up and sent them back one by one.

The meatballs were fun by themselves too. I juggled them. I invented games like "roll the meatball across the table" and "obstacle-course meatball golf." My brother and I played catch with meatballs. There's one special game of meatball catch that I'd like to tell you about.

I grew up in the Bronx, New York, within walking distance of one of the most famous ballparks in America, Yankee Stadium. So it was only natural that I was a big Yankees fan when I was a kid. One day, when I was nine or ten years old and my brother was about five, we were in the kitchen. At that time we lived on the top floor of a six-story apartment house overlooking the street. It was a very hot summer day, and we didn't have air conditioning. I don't think anybody did, at least not in my neighborhood. Because it was so hot, the kitchen window was open. There was a grate with a little fence in front of it so we couldn't fall out. Anyhow, I got hold of a meatball and decided to play catch with my brother.

I pretended to be Whitey Ford, a famous and fabulous pitcher for the Yankees, and my brother pretended to be Yogi Berra, an equally famous and fabulous catcher. He crouched down in front of the window at one end of the kitchen, and I held up the meatball at the other end. I said something like "Okay, kid, I'm going to show you my sidearm curve." I wound up and flung the meatball as hard as I could in my brother's direction. The pitch was a little high, he couldn't catch it, and the meatball went sailing out the window.

At that very moment, six floors below, a man was driving by in a convertible . . . with the top down. We could hear him jam on the brakes as a meatball, apparently from outer space, landed in his lap. He probably scratched his head and stared at the meatball, saying something like "That's a meatball! Where did the meatball come from? Where did the meatball come from?" He jumped out of the car, looked around, saw my brother and me at the open window, and yelled, "Hey! What's going on up there?" My kid brother and I made funny faces, wiggled our hands, and yelled back at him, "Meatball attack!"

Needless to say, my mother did not approve of that sort of behavior, and she had a whole list of rules about things that my brother and I were not supposed to do with food. More than thirty years later I made a list of as many of her food rules as I could remember, added a few of my own, and wrote a poem called "My Mother Says I'm Sickening."

My Mother Says I'm Sickening

My mother says I'm sickening,
my mother says I'm crude,
she says this when she sees me
playing Ping-Pong with my food,
she doesn't seem to like it
when I slurp my bowl of stew,
and now she's got a list of things
she says I mustn't do—

DO NOT CATAPULT THE CARROTS!
DO NOT JUGGLE GOBS OF FAT!
DO NOT DROP THE MASHED POTATOES
ON THE GERBIL OR THE CAT!
NEVER PUNCH THE PUMPKIN PUDDING!
NEVER TUNNEL THROUGH THE BREAD!

PUT NO PEAS INTO YOUR POCKET!
PLACE NO NOODLES ON YOUR HEAD!
DO NOT SQUEEZE THE STEAMED ZUCCHINI!
DO NOT MAKE THE MELON OOZE!
NEVER STUFF VANILLA YOGURT
IN YOUR LITTLE SISTER'S SHOES!
DRAW NO FACES IN THE KETCHUP!
MAKE NO LITTLE GRAVY POOLS!

I wish my mother wouldn't make
so many useless rules.

My mother had another sort of rule about food. I think that a lot of mothers have this particular rule: If it was on your plate, you ate it. If you didn't eat it, it would be on your plate at the next meal. If you didn't eat it then, it would be there at the next meal too. This sometimes went on for days. Of course food does get weird after a while, and my mother realized that I was never going to eat it, but she couldn't bear to throw it out. She had a solution. My mother designated a space in the refrigerator, about a square foot, second shelf down in the back on the right side, for food that was too old to eat but wasn't quite old enough to throw out. She kept it there until it was weird enough and old enough to throw out.

I love writing poems about things that really happened to me when I was a kid, so I wrote a poem about that space in the refrigerator. Of course I exaggerate a bit—a poet is allowed to do that—but the basic story is true. The poem is called "Deep in Our Refrigerator."

Deep in Our Refrigerator

Deep in our refrigerator,
there's a special place
for food that's been around awhile . . .
we keep it, just in case.
"It's probably too old to eat,"
my mother likes to say.
"But I don't think it's old enough
for me to throw away."

It stays there for a month or more
to ripen in the cold,
and soon we notice fuzzy clumps
of multicolored mold.
The clumps are larger every day,
we notice this as well,
but mostly what we notice
is a certain special smell.

When finally it all becomes
a nasty mess of slime,
my mother takes it out, and says,
"Apparently, it's time."
She dumps it in the garbage can,
though not without regret,
then fills that space with other food
that's not so ancient yet.

Write about things that really happened to you; it's one of the best ways to get started as a poet. Does your mother have rules? Of course she does. Do those rules drive you crazy? Of course they do. Write about your mother's rules and why you think they're good or bad and why they drive you crazy.

Does your mother have little quirks? Of course she does. One of my mother's quirks was saving inedible food until it was old enough to throw out. That's kind of nutty when you think about it, but lots of people do it, and my mother was one of them. Maybe your mother does it too. Or maybe she has another quirk, like never throwing out a piece of string, no matter how small and useless, or arranging all the food in the pantry in alphabetical order, or washing a bar of soap after she uses it.

You can write about any of these things. Once you start thinking about them, you'll find it hard to stop. If you don't want people to know that you're writing about your mother, then change her name, or pretend it's someone else's mother, or change her into an animal—even a bug. It's completely up to you.

My Baby Brother

I can't say this often enough: *Write what you know.* One thing that I know very well and have written about often is my little brother. He's bigger than I am now, but it wasn't always that way.

Until my brother was born, I was the only kid in the house, so of course I was considered *special*! That's right, I was wonderful. I was amazing. I was incredible. I was sensational.

I was a genius! It didn't matter what I did, my mother would still brag about me. "Oh, look, my son the genius is sleeping with his face in the oatmeal again."

That all changed when I was not quite five years old, and my mother brought home a weird-looking little package from the hospital—my baby brother. I hated him! I hated him because all of a sudden my parents seemed to forget all about me, and I wasn't so special anymore. Now, to be fair, I have to admit that my mother tried to make me feel better about him at first. She handed him to me, all wrapped up snugly in a blue blanket. With a big smile and looking more enthusiastic than I'd ever seen her before, she said, "Son, this is yours!" I guess she supposed I'd like him better if I thought that he was a present for me.

I took a good look at him. What an ugly little critter! He had a tiny, wrinkled face and more or less resembled a cross between a prune and a peeled armadillo. I couldn't believe that I was related to this creature. I wrinkled up my own face, shook my head, and said to my mother, "This—this *thing* is *mine*? I don't think so. Uh-uh. No way," and I handed him right back.

As he grew older, I got to like him more, but at first I didn't find him all that interesting. After all, he didn't do much of anything. Mostly he slept, and when he wasn't sleeping, he cried, and when he wasn't crying, he wiggled around a bit. His major occupations seemed to be peeing and pooping in his diaper. He was a smelly little guy.

Over the years I've written many poems

about my brother or based on him. Here's a poem about my brother when he was just a week old. The poem is very simple and says in very few words what he was like when I was not quite five years old and saw him for the first time.

My Baby Brother

My baby brother is so small,
he hasn't even learned to crawl.
He's only been around a week,
and all he seems to do is bawl
and wiggle, sleep . . . and leak.

Do you have a brother or a sister? If you do, try writing a poem about him or her. If you have more than one, write about all of them. If you don't, then try writing about your friends and about their brothers and sisters. Ask your friends questions about them. If you have a dog or cat or other pet, write about it. I absolutely always advise beginning poets to start out by writing about what they know, and I think that you all know a lot about your siblings and your pets.

Also, a poem doesn't have to be long. There's nothing wrong with a long poem, but don't make your poem long just for the sake of doing it. If those extra lines don't add anything to what you want to say, take them out.

A long time ago I wrote a poem about oysters. In the poem I said in six words everything that I wanted to say about oysters. I suppose that I could have made the poem longer, but I don't think that making it longer would have made it better. In fact I'm positive that making it longer would have made it worse.

Here's the poem: ➝

Oysters

O ysters are creatures without any features.

Years later I thought of more things to say about oysters and wrote a somewhat longer poem about them. It's called "Do Oysters Sneeze?" Just because you've written one poem about something doesn't mean you can't write another poem or another dozen poems about the same subject. Maybe someday I'll write another oyster poem, but I won't write it if I don't have something else to say about oysters that I haven't said before. Try to think of new things to say about something you've written about previously. If you can't think of anything new about that subject, then write about something else. I do it all the time. Here's that other oyster poem:

🐸 🐸 🐸

Do Oysters Sneeze?

Do oysters sneeze beneath the seas,
or wiggle to and fro,
or sulk, or smile, or dance awhile
. . . how can we ever know?

Do oysters yawn when roused at dawn,
and do they ever weep,
and can we tell, when, in its shell,
an oyster is asleep?

Performing Bananas and Flying Hot Dogs

Ideas for poems happen at unpredictable times, in unpredictable places, and in unpredictable ways. For example, a long time ago a friend gave me a greeting card with a picture of a dancing banana on the front. It was a funny card, but I didn't think too much about it at the time, though I did jot down something about it in my notebook. Several years later the card turned up again, and I thought: Hmm . . . a dancing banana. There might be a poem in this.

I worked on the poem off and on for several days, and the dancing banana soon turned into a *singing* and dancing banana. That seemed funnier and more interesting to me. The single singing and dancing banana soon became a duet and then a trio. I worked on the poem some more and decided to put a few banana puns into it. Also, I changed *singing and dancing bananas* to *performing bananas.* Once I had the word *performing*, I realized that four was a better number than three for my bananas, as it reinforced the *for* sound in *performing.* As the poem developed, I changed *four* to *forty.* I had two reasons for this. First, *forty* worked better for the scansion of the poem, and second, forty performing bananas seemed a lot wackier and more wonderful than just four.

I thought about the poem some more and decided that it would be fun to put as many banana puns into the poem as I could. I wrote down things like *banana splits, banana belt, top banana*, and more and figured out ways of using these puns in the poem so that they seemed to belong and *had* to be there. I must have rewritten "Forty Performing Bananas" a hundred times, but I think that it was worth all the work.

Forty Performing Bananas

We're FORTY PERFORMING BANANAS,
in bright yellow slippery skins,
our features are rather appealing,
though we've neither shoulders nor chins,
we cha-cha, fandango, and tango,
we lick and we skip and we hop,
while half of us belt out a ballad,
the rest of us spin like a top.

We're FORTY PERFORMING BANANAS,
we mambo, we samba, we waltz,
we dangle and swing from the ceiling,
then turn very slick somersaults,
people drive here in bunches to see us,
our splits earn us worldly renown,
we're FORTY PERFORMING BANANAS,
come see us when you are in town.

When I was working on my book *Something Big Has Been Here*, I thought that I might write another food poem that was filled with puns, but I couldn't decide what that food should be. One day I was in a novelty store, the sort of place that sells plastic barf and hot-pepper chewing gum. I bought a little plastic foam glider in the shape of a hot dog. "What a great idea," I said to myself. "A flying hot dog!" I knew that I had found a subject for my next big food poem. By the way, I also bought a flying hamburger and flying french fries, but so far they haven't resulted in poems.

Once again I took out my notebook and made a list. This time I listed all the hot dog puns I could think of, some of which are obvious and some of which are hidden in the poem. I thought of many more hot dog puns than I had banana puns. As the poem progressed, I decided to change that single flying hot dog to *five* flying hot dogs, a sort of mini-squadron. I wrote the poem in the voice of the squadron leader, whom I like to think of as Major Wiener. He boasts about his aeronautical exploits and those of his fellow squadron members. I worked on this poem off and on for more than a year but couldn't figure out a way to finish it. I wrote and rewrote the poem *several hundred times*, but I still couldn't come up with a satisfactory ending.

voice: in poetry, the narrator of the poem. On a broader scale, *voice* can also refer to the unique style found in a particular writer's work. In this case, *voice* is something writers want to achieve, and often it requires a lot of writing to find it.

I put the poem aside for a couple of months and didn't think about it at all. Then one morning I suddenly woke with a big grin on my face. The ending and a couple of other missing pieces had come to me in my sleep. I sat up in bed, opened my notebook, and finished the poem right there and then. It's called "We're Fearless Flying Hot Dogs," and it's one of the most difficult poems I've written. It's also one of my favorites.

We're Fearless
Flying Hot Dogs

We're fearless flying hot dogs,
the famous "Unflappable Five,"
we're mustered in formation
to climb, to dip, to dive,
we spread our wings with relish,
then reach for altitude,
we're aerobatic wieners,
the fastest flying food.

(continued)

We're fearless flying hot dogs,
we race with flair and style,
then catch up with each other
and soar in single file,
you never saw such daring,
such power and control,
as when we swoop and spiral,
then slide into a roll.

The throngs applaud our antics,
they cheer us long and loud,
there's never a chilly reception,
there's never a sour crowd,
and if we may speak frankly,
we are a thrilling sight,
we're fearless flying hot dogs,
the delicate essence of flight.

I *always* carry a notebook and a couple of pens. If I don't write down my ideas immediately, there's almost a 100 percent chance that I'll forget them. As soon as I saw that dancing-banana card, I wrote down my idea. It was the same in the novelty store. That flying hot dog poem would not exist if I hadn't written down my idea for the poem at once.

Another very important thing about writing is *rewriting*. I doubt that I've ever written a poem that came out exactly right the first time. Every poem I write gets rewritten at least once, and most get rewritten half a dozen times or more. As I said, I rewrote that hot dog poem several hundred times. I don't expect you to do that, but you should look closely at what you've written and ask yourself if there's a way that you could improve it. I ask myself that question a lot, and the answer is always yes! Sometimes there are whole sections or lines of a poem that can be made better, and sometimes it's just a matter of a single word.

Many years ago I wrote a poem about a fire-eater. I had him swallowing all sorts of embers and coals but couldn't quite find the word I wanted to have him finish his hot meal. I decided that it would be fitting to wash down all that fire with lemonade but still couldn't find the perfect verb. That's when I went to a book I *always* have on my desk, a thesaurus. It's probably my most useful reference book and has helped me solve problems thousands of times. Eventually I found the word that I was looking for. The word is *extinguish*. Once I saw it in the thesaurus, it seemed obvious. I strongly suggest that you keep a

thesaurus: a special kind of dictionary that groups words with the same meaning. Suppose you're looking for another word for *big*. In the thesaurus you'll find that similar words are *large, great, huge, enormous,* and so on. This is a very useful book for writers. You should be able to find one in your school or public library.

rhyming dictionary: a reference book that lists more rhymes than you could possibly think of. I find it invaluable. You should be able to find one in your school or public library.

thesaurus around when you're writing, whether it's poetry or prose. A rhyming dictionary helps too.

More Bananas

One day I was taking a walk in Seattle, and I crossed a bridge. On the far side of the bridge a man had set up a small, impromptu fruit stand where he was selling bananas. Bananas happen to be a personal favorite, and I eat one almost every day. I bought some bananas from the man, peeled one, and started eating it. That's when an idea occurred to me, one that had never occurred to me before. The letter *B* at the beginning of the word *bridge* and the letter *B* at the beginning of the word *banana* blended together in my brain. I started thinking about building a bridge out of bananas. This is interesting! I thought. Now, I know that I'm not actually going to build a bridge out of bananas, but I see no reason why I can't write a poem about building a bridge out of bananas. I mean, after all, a bridge built out of bananas wouldn't work in the real world, but it could certainly work as the subject of a poem. So I took out my notebook, made a few notes, and then began working on the poem.

℮ WRITING TIP #5 ℮ ℮ ℮ ℮ ℮ ℮ ℮

When I began the poem, I had no idea what I was going to do with it. Furthermore, I had no idea how I was going to end the poem. This happens a lot. Sometimes I have the ending of a poem in my head and have to backtrack in order to get to that ending. Sometimes I have the middle of a poem in my head and have to figure out the beginning *and* the end. Sometimes I have nothing more than a couple of rhyming lines or just a couple of words in my head and have to figure out how to build a poem out of that. And sometimes, as in this case, I have the beginning but have no idea how to end the poem.

As I worked on the poem and thought more and more about bananas, I asked myself why a bridge built out of bananas wouldn't work. The answers were obvious: Bananas are too soft, they're not strong enough, they get even softer and eventually get rotten, and so on. Let's face it, a bridge built out of bananas is going to fall down pretty quickly.

Eventually a way to end the poem popped into my head. The same thing can happen when you write a poem. Keep thinking and thinking about your subject, and more often than not, the ending will occur to you.

I'm Building
a Bridge of Bananas

I'm building a bridge of bananas,
it's pretty, but not very strong.
Bananas are not very sturdy,
bananas don't last very long.
Initially green, and then yellow,
increasingly speckled with brown,
inevitably, as they ripen,
it's clear that my bridge will fall down.

(continued)

My bridge is developing fissures
and even some sizable gaps.
It's senseless to try and repair it,
I might as well let it collapse.
It waggles and sags in the middle,
it wobbles and droops at the ends,
and so I've alerted my neighbors,
as well as my family and friends.

They're trucking in freezers of ice cream
of every last flavor that's made,
plus whipped cream and chocolate syrup,
both of a premium grade.
They're bringing me barrels of walnuts,
and cherries without any pits—
we'll shortly be sharing delicious
gigantic banana bridge splits.

My Teddy Bear

Sometimes ideas for poems surface while I'm doing a perfectly ordinary thing in a perfectly ordinary place. Here's an example: I was sitting in a restaurant in El Paso, Texas, having a quiet dinner by myself, when I became aware of a disturbance at the next table. A little boy about four years old was very angry about something, I don't know what, and he was screaming at the top of his lungs. Also, he was taking his rage out on his teddy bear. He was twisting it; he was biting its nose; he was biting its eyes; he was banging it on the table; he was trying to tear out its stuffing. He was jabbing it with his fork! He was absolutely inconsolable and continued doing as much damage to his teddy bear as he possibly could.

As I watched him, it reminded me of my own teddy bear, which I loved when I was a little boy. It also reminded me of how I used to knock it around and twist it when I was upset. I don't know why I took out my anger on my innocent teddy bear, but I did. I suspect that lots of kids do.

When I was about six years old, my teddy bear suddenly disappeared. I asked my mother about it, but she pretended not to know. Many years later I discovered that she'd given it to my cousin, who was a few years younger than I was. Many years after that, I learned that when he was in the air force, he kept that teddy bear in the cockpit of his plane as a good-luck charm. I'd like to have my teddy bear back, but he won't give it to me.

On the basis of that experience in the restaurant, I wrote a poem called "Oh, Teddy Bear." Here it is:

Oh, Teddy Bear

Oh, Teddy Bear, dear Teddy,
though you're gone these many years,
I recall with deep affection
how I nibbled on your ears,
I can hardly keep from smiling,
and my heart beats fast and glows,
when I think about the morning
when I twisted off your nose.

Teddy Bear, you didn't whimper,
Teddy Bear, you didn't pout,
when I reached in with my fingers
and I tore your tummy out,
and you didn't even mumble
or emit the faintest cries,
when I pulled your little paws off,
when I bit your button eyes.

Yes, you sat beside me calmly,
and you didn't once protest,
when I ripped apart the stuffing
that was packed inside your chest,
and you didn't seem to notice
when I yanked out all your hair—
it's been ages since I've seen you,
but I miss you, Teddy Bear.

I've shared this poem with thousands and thousands of kids in schools all over the United States and in other countries. Then I've asked them to tell me what *they* did to their *own* teddy bears or other favorite stuffed toys. I've gotten the most remarkable answers, many of which I never would have thought of myself. One little boy said, "I gave my teddy bear a haircut. I thought it would grow back, but I was wrong." A little girl outdid him when she said, "I shaved my teddy bear with shaving cream and my father's electric razor." I've discovered that a lot of kids have cooked their teddy bears. Boys and girls have told me that they've steamed their bears, fried their bears, baked their bears, and boiled their bears. One of my favorites is the boy who told me in a rich Southern drawl, "Ah barbecued mah bear."

I especially remember one boy who had a sort of squeaky voice. He said, "When I was little, I had just learned to flush the toilet. I was so proud. I wanted to show my teddy bear that I knew how to flush the toilet, so I took him with me into the bathroom and said, 'Look, teddy bear, I can flush the toilet.' But I accidentally dropped him in. There was nothing I could do. I never saw my teddy bear again."

Most kids have had a teddy bear or other stuffed toy that they loved. Try writing a poem about one of your favorite toys, stuffed or otherwise. Make a list of everything you can remember about that toy and then start exaggerating. That's what I did in my own teddy bear poem. If you can't remember enough about it, ask your friends about their stuffed toys. Maybe you'll hear something so wonderful that you simply have to put it in a poem. There's no law that says you can't combine something that you did with something someone else did. I do it all the time.

Another thing is to be aware of what's going on around you. If I hadn't paid attention to that little boy in the restaurant in Texas, I never would have written the poem. And remember, as soon as you notice something special or as soon as you get an idea, *write it down.* I'm never without a notebook, and I make notes in it almost every day. I've been filling notebooks with ideas for more than forty years, and I have so many that if I stacked them up, they'd be at least twice as tall as I am. I still haven't used all the ideas in those notebooks.

By the way, I wrote another teddy bear poem based on that little boy who told me that he gave his teddy bear a haircut, thinking that it would grow back. Here it is:

My Brother Shaved
His Teddy Bear

My brother shaved his Teddy Bear
about a year ago,
he did a very thorough job
and stripped it, head to toe.
He acted sort of suddenly,
entirely on a whim.
It sounds a bit unusual . . .
it's normal though, for him.

Before my brother shaved it,
it was quite a handsome bear,
but now it looks pathetic
and appears beyond repair.
Its fur was soft and velvety,
luxurious and long.
He thought it would grow back again—
it looks like he was wrong.

Meat Loaf and Turkey

There's another thing that I'd like to tell you about my mother. She was a terrible cook. Okay, she wasn't *that* terrible, but she wasn't very good. There were basically two reasons for this: (1) She didn't know how to cook, and (2) She was absentminded. The first reason is self-explanatory. The second needs a bit more explanation. You see, my mother forgot things when she cooked. For example, she sometimes added salt to a dish three times, forgetting that she'd added salt twice before. She might forget that there were vegetables boiling on the stove. By the time she remembered, there'd be nothing but a soggy gray mess in the pot.

Once my mother prepared a meat loaf and put it in the oven. About an hour later she forgot that it was in there and took us to visit my grandma. By the way, my grandma was a fabulous cook, and I've often wondered why that didn't rub off on my mother. Anyhow, when we returned home several hours later, the kitchen was full of thick, dark smoke. "Oh, no, my meat loaf!" my mother shrieked. She turned off the oven and opened every window in our apartment. It took most of the evening for the smoke to clear. Of course the meat loaf was burned to a crisp. It was a charred, inedible blob, and we ended up having cereal for supper.

When I was working on a book, I remembered my mother's meat loaf and wrote a poem based on it. It's called "My Mother Made a Meat Loaf." After you read the poem, I'll tell you a bit about some of the techniques I used to write it.

My Mother Made a Meat Loaf

My mother made a meat loaf
that provided much distress,
she tried her best to serve it,
but she met with no success,
her sharpest knife was powerless
to cut a single slice,
and her efforts with a cleaver
failed completely to suffice.

She whacked it with a hammer,
and she smacked it with a brick,
but she couldn't faze that meat loaf,
it remained without a nick,
I decided I would help her
and assailed it with a drill,
but the drill made no impression,
though I worked with all my skill.

We chipped at it with chisels,
but we didn't make a dent,
it appeared my mother's meat loaf
was much harder than cement,
then we set upon that meat loaf
with a hatchet and an ax,
but that meat loaf stayed unblemished
and withstood our fierce attacks.

We borrowed bows and arrows,
and we fired at close range,
it didn't make a difference,
for that meat loaf didn't change,
we beset it with a blowtorch,
but we couldn't find a flaw,
and we both were flabbergasted
when it broke the power saw.

(continued)

We hired a hippopotamus
to trample it around,
but that meat loaf was so mighty
that it simply stood its ground,
now we manufacture meat loaves
by the millions, all year long,
they are famous in construction,
building houses tall and strong.

It can be captivating to write a poem based on something that really happened, then add your own personal stamp to it. To write "My Mother Made a Meat Loaf," I started with the memory of my mother's ruined meat loaf and used that as my premise. At the time I was living in New Mexico in an adobe house, and the adobe bricks reminded me of the meat loaf. Now I knew, more or less, how I would end the poem. I would compare her meat loaf with a brick. Once again, I took out my trusty notebook and made a list. I listed all the ways that I could try to cut a meat loaf that was as hard as a brick. Making a list is one of the best ways to make sure that you have enough material for your poem. Many of my poems begin with a list, and so can yours. As the poem progressed, I found that it worked best if I kept exaggerating more and more. At first the meat loaf can't be cut with a knife, then it's impervious to an ax, and finally even a hippopotamus can't trample it. This is another great technique. Keep making things weirder and weirder or sillier and sillier or more and more impossible.

Here's another idea. Look at a poem you've written, and ask yourself, "Can I write a poem that's the *opposite* of this one?" Very often you can. In this case I'd just written a poem about the world's hardest food, my mother's indestructible meat loaf. Now I decided to turn the idea upside down and write one about the world's *softest* food. I thought about lots of soft foods, things like applesauce and mashed potatoes. Though I tried and tried, I couldn't think of a funny idea for a poem. Yet I didn't give up.

Eventually I had a brainstorm. I'd write a poem about food that had exploded–that's how it would get soft. Now I had to think of what food to choose and how to make it explode. I thought and thought and settled on the notion of an exploding turkey, and I had a really silly way to make that turkey explode. Sometimes you just have to keep thinking. Remember, one idea leads to another. Here's the poem:

The Turkey Shot Out
of the Oven

The turkey shot out of the oven
and rocketed into the air,
it knocked every plate off the table
and partly demolished a chair.

It ricocheted into a corner
and burst with a deafening boom,
then splattered all over the kitchen,
completely obscuring the room.

It stuck to the walls and the windows,
it totally coated the floor,
there was turkey attached the ceiling,
where there'd never been turkey before.

It blanketed every appliance,
it smeared every saucer and bowl,
there wasn't a way I could stop it,
that turkey was out of control.

I scraped and I scrubbed with displeasure,
and thought with chagrin as I mopped,
that I'd never again stuff a turkey
with popcorn that hadn't been popped.

An Awful, Awful Meal

I arrived in a small town in southern New Mexico around noon one Sunday. The restaurant at the motel where I was staying wasn't open on Sunday, and neither were any other restaurants in the vicinity. I was hungry, so I asked several people if there was a place within walking distance where I could get a good meal. They all recommended the same place, a diner about a mile or so away. A half hour later I was sitting in a booth in that diner, poring over the menu. The place was full, so it took a while for a waitress to take my order and even longer before I was served. I ordered some juice, a steak, mashed potatoes with gravy, mixed vegetables, a cup of coffee, and a slice of apple pie. As I said, I was hungry. While I waited, I looked around and saw that everyone else in the diner seemed to be enjoying his or her lunch.

By the time my meal finally arrived, I was positively famished and looked forward to eating every single bite that was put in front of me. The first thing about my lunch that I noticed was that the juice was warm. Also, it had an odd, unpleasant taste, and I decided not to drink it. I tasted the mashed potatoes. They were lumpy, and the gravy tasted even more unpleasant than the juice. The vegetables were such an unattractive mess and looked so unappetizing that I couldn't bring myself to sample them. After some effort, I managed to cut a piece off the overdone steak but noted with dismay that it was practically inedible. It had the consistency of cardboard and an unsavory flavor; also it hurt my teeth and jaw when I tried to chew it. There was bread on a side plate, but that was stale and had bits of mold on it.

I decided to skip the main course and try the dessert—but no luck there. The pie managed to be tasteless, tough, and mushy all at the same time, and the coffee was cold and weird. Even though I went into that diner hungry, I went out hungry. I simply couldn't bear to eat that meal. However, as I mentioned, I observed that everyone else there was eating his or her meal with relish. I guess that they'd simply gotten used to it.

Lunch was not a total loss, however, because I took out my notebook and made extensive notes about it and then wrote a poem based on it. Here it is: ➡

Gussie's Greasy Spoon

Every day, at ten past noon,
I enter GUSSIE'S GREASY SPOON,
I plop down in the nearest seat,
and order food unfit to eat.
I try the juice, it's warm and vile,
the scrambled eggs are green as bile,
the beets are blue, the beans are gray,
the cauliflower tastes like clay.

At GUSSIE'S GREASY SPOON, the stew
is part cement, part hay, part glue,
it's mostly gristle, ropy tough,
a tiger couldn't chew the stuff.
The rancid soup is foul and thin,
a bit like bitter medicine,
the melon smells, the salad sags,
the mashed potatoes seem like rags.

One whiff of Gussie's weird cuisine
makes stomachs ache, turns faces green,
her moldy muffins have no peers,
they'll make you sick for forty years.
The coffee's cold, the cake is stale,
the doughnuts taste like pickled whale,
yet, every day, at ten past noon,
I eat at GUSSIE'S GREASY SPOON.

WRITING TIP #8

I never pass up an opportunity to write a poem. Poems do not have to be based on *good* experiences; they can be based on bad ones too. Try writing a poem about something awful or unpleasant that happened to you. Bad things happen to everyone. Maybe you got hit in the nose with a baseball, or fell out of a tree, or had your bicycle stolen, or were scratched by a deranged cat, or got a terrible stomachache after a meal. Actually, all of these things (and many more) have happened to me, and I've made notes about them. Perhaps I'll write poems about some or even all of these experiences.

Sit down, open your notebook, take out your pen or pencil, and list as many unpleasant things that have happened to you as you can. You'll be amazed at how many there are. Of course you can also list things that have happened to *other* people, including your friends, family, neighbors, and schoolmates. As always, you can make things up. Pick one of the items on your list, write down *everything* you can think of about it, and then try to put it into a poem. Remember, you're allowed to exaggerate . . . and I hope that you do.

There's Something About Pigs

There are some things that I keep writing about. I'm not exactly sure why; it just seems to work out that way. Pigs are animals that I return to again and again in my poetry, and so far I haven't run out of things to say about them. Maybe it's the way they look, or their reputation, or the sounds they make, or their eating habits, or any number of other things. It's probably

some combination of things. In any event,
I enjoy writing about them. Here's a pig
poem: ⟶

A Piglet

I'm a piglet, pink and stout.
If I'm cold, I sneeze and sniff.
If I have to blow my snout,
I take out my oinkerchief.

I got the idea for a poem in the parlor of a bed-and-breakfast inn that I was staying at in Connecticut. The inn was famous for its ham, and there were several hams hanging overhead. The room was also decorated with little pig statuettes. I happened to have a cold and had to take out my handkerchief to blow my nose. That's when I put the whole business of the poem together. I substituted *oink* for *hand* in the word *handkerchief*, and worked backward from there. That's really the whole secret of the poem. It wouldn't have worked at all if I'd ended with the word *handkerchief*. It's that little surprise at the end that does the trick.

For another poem about a pig I used the word *oink* as a pun, changing *ointment* to *oinkment*. I think it works just as well as *oinkerchief,* maybe even a bit better, because *oinkment* looks and sounds more like *ointment* than *oinkerchief* looks and sounds like *handkerchief.* I'll leave it up to you to decide. Here's the poem: ⟶

My Pig Put On
a Bathing Suit

My pig put on a bathing suit
and headed for the shore,
then sat beneath the blazing sun
from ten till ten to four.

Of course it soon was sunburned,
all its tender skin was sore.
I covered it with *oinkment* . . .
my pig is sore no more.

ℰ WRITING TIP #9 ℯ ℯ ℯ ℯ ℯ ℯ ℯ

The more you write, the more you may find yourself drawn to certain topics. Maybe you'll especially like writing about your family or your pets. Maybe you'll have the most to say about your friends or relatives. Maybe you'll write about bugs or planets or baseball or maybe about baseball-playing bugs on other planets.

That's another reason to carry a notebook. Whenever you think of something new about your favorite subject—your dog, for example— write it down *immediately*. You probably won't use all the ideas you jot down in a single poem, but sooner or later you're likely to use some of them in one poem and some of them in another poem. You can never make too many notes. Many of my pig poems would never have happened if I'd stopped writing down ideas about pigs after I'd written my first pig poem. I still occasionally jot down something new about pigs.

The Bogeyman

As I've mentioned before, I was not the best-behaved little boy in the world, and I often disobeyed my mother. When I was about three or four years old, she figured out a clever way to get me to do things. For example, let's say that I was playing outside and my mother wanted me to come in for supper. She'd call to me out the window, "Jack, come on in, it's time for supper." I pretended that I hadn't heard her and simply went on doing what I was doing. So she called out a little louder. "Oh, maybe you didn't hear me. I said come on in, it's time for supper."

This time I answered her: "No! I want to stay out here and play."

So then she said even louder, "I said come in, it's time for supper."

"No!" I insisted.

My mother yelled, "You're making me mad!"

"I don't care," I said.

Then she made her voice so soft that it was hard to hear her. "If you don't come in right now, the *bogeyman's* going to get you."

"Okay," I said. "I'll be right in."

When I was inside, my mother said, "Wash your hands." I ignored her. So she said, "Oh, maybe you didn't hear me. I said wash your hands."

"No!" I said.

"I said wash your hands," she said a bit louder.

"No!" I said. "They're only going to get dirty again."

"You're making me mad," she said.

"I don't care," I said.

Then she made her voice soft again and said, "You wash your hands or the *bogeyman's* going to get you!"

"Okay," I said, and washed my hands.

At dinner I always ate the meat first and then, if there was any room left, the potatoes. I almost never touched the vegetables.

"Eat your vegetables," my mother said. I pretended that I didn't hear her.

"Oh, maybe you didn't hear me. I said eat your vegetables."

"No!"

"Eat your vegetables," she said a bit louder.

"No!" I said. "I don't like them, and you can't make me eat them."

"You're making me mad," she said.

"I don't care."

Then her voice got very soft, and she said, almost in a whisper, "You eat your vegetables or the *bogeyman's* going to get you."

"Okay," I said, and ate my vegetables in a hurry.

Later in the evening my mother said, "It's bedtime. Put on your pajamas and get ready for bed." I pretended that I didn't hear her.

"Oh, maybe you didn't hear me," my

mother said. "I told you to put on your pajamas and get ready for bed."

"No!"

"Go to bed," she said a bit louder.

"No, I don't want to go to bed. I'm not tired."

"I said, go to bed."

"No! You're so mean."

Her voice got very soft, and she said, "You go to bed or the *bogeyman's* going to get you."

"Okay, I'll go to bed." And I did.

This sort of thing went on for a long time until I finally figured out that no matter what I did or didn't do, the bogeyman never got me. So I decided to play a little trick on my mother. I woke up in the middle of the night and started screaming at the top of my voice, "Help! Help! Mommy! Mommy! Mommy! The bogeyman! The bogeyman! He's got me! He's biting me! He's chewing me! He's eating me! Help! Help! Mommy! Mommy! Mommy!"

I guess I must have scared my mother half out of her wits. She raced down the hall, charged into my bedroom, and switched on the light, all the while shouting, "Oh! My boy! My boy! My poor little boy! What's the matter? What's the matter? What's the matter?"

And there I was, standing up in the middle of my bed with an enormous grin on my face. "I fooled you!" I said to her.

After that my mother never threatened me with the bogeyman again. Also, I didn't have any dessert for the next two weeks.

🐛 WRITING TIP #10 🐛 🐛 🐛 🐛 🐛 🐛 🐛

When I worked on my book *Nightmares*, the first poem that I wrote was "The Bogeyman," because that was the creature I remembered most vividly from my own childhood. I decided that having the bogeyman come to my house was a bit too scary, so I put my bogeyman in a remote and dreadful location. As long as you don't go there, you're all right, but if you do go there . . . well, that's another matter entirely. That's one of the things about writing poetry: You're always free to change whatever you want. You can change the place, the time, and the events—and of course you can add or subtract whatever you want.

If the creature you have in mind isn't as big as you want it to be, make it bigger. If it's too big for your purposes, make it smaller. Alter its shape and color and hairstyle. The only limitation is your own imagination. That's part of the power of the creative process.

The Bogeyman

In the desolate depths of a perilous place
the bogeyman lurks, with a snarl on his face.
Never dare, never dare to approach his dark lair
for he's waiting . . . just waiting . . . to get you.

He skulks in the shadows, relentless and wild
in his search for a tender, delectable child.
With his steely sharp claws and his slavering jaws
oh he's waiting . . . just waiting . . . to get you.

Many have entered his dreary domain
but not even one has been heard from again.
They no doubt made a feast for the butchering
    beast
and he's waiting . . . just waiting . . . to get you.

In that sulphurous, sunless and sinister place
he'll crumple your bones in his bogey embrace.
Never never go near if you hold your life dear,
for oh! . . . what he'll do . . . when he gets you!

It Doesn't
Have
to Rhyme

Sometimes when I'm having problems getting a poem to rhyme, I sit down and write a few haiku. I enjoy writing them so much that I decided to do a whole book of them. Here's a poem from it:

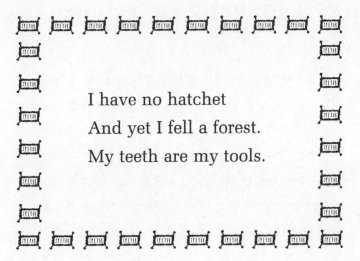

I have no hatchet
And yet I fell a forest.
My teeth are my tools.

You've probably figured out that it's a
beaver doing the talking.

℮ WRITING TIP #11 ℮ ℮ ℮ ℮ ℮ ℮ ℮

In case you didn't already know this, here's a little secret about writing poetry that rhymes: It's hard. Sometimes I simply can't come up with the perfect rhyme, even if I use a rhyming dictionary, an extremely useful and valuable book.

Every once in a while I decide to write poetry that doesn't rhyme. Haiku was invented in Japan and is a special kind of unrhymed poetry. Traditional haiku has three lines. The first line has five syllables, the second line has seven syllables, and the third has five syllables, adding up to a total of seventeen syllables. Haiku is usually written about a single thing or event in nature, such as a cricket, the wind blowing through the grass, or the last leaf on a tree. Many poets

☀ **104** PIZZA, PIGS, AND POETRY

writing in English have found that it's a useful form for expressing insights about ordinary life. It's also generally written from the poet's point of view.

When I wrote my book of haiku, I decided to write each poem from the animal's point of view instead. That means I pretended I was the animal speaking. That's what I did with the beaver haiku and with all the others in the book.

Pick an animal—it can be a bird, bug, fish, reptile, or mammal—and write a haiku about it. You can write it in the creature's voice or in your own. Keep looking for ways to make your poem better. The shorter the poem, the more important each word becomes.

Written in Concrete

One time my editor called and asked me to write her a poem in a circle. I wasn't sure what she meant, and I asked her to explain. She recited one of her favorite poems that she remembered from her childhood. The poem was in the shape of a circle, and it didn't have an end because the last line went directly into the first line, and the poem could keep going forever.

"I don't think that I can write a poem like that," I told her.

"How do you know?" she asked.

"I've never done it," I replied.

She answered me with one word: "Try."

I said that I would, and even though I was pretty sure that I couldn't do it, she expressed a lot of confidence in me and told me that she'd be surprised if I didn't come up with something.

When I hung up the phone, I took a piece of paper, drew a circle on it, and made a few notes around the circle. Then I had a happy accident. I dropped the paper, and when I bent down to pick it up, practically the whole poem popped right into my head. I would write a poem about walking in a circle and picking up a piece of paper that had some writing on it.

Ten minutes later I called my editor back
and read her my poem. She was astonished,
and she loved it. Here's the poem:

I Was Walking in a Circle

I WAS WALKING IN A CIRCLE WHEN I SPIED A PIECE OF PAPER COVERED WITH A PRETTY PICTURE COLORED YELLOW GREEN AND RED AS I PICKED IT UP I NOTICED THAT IT ALSO HAD SOME WRITING AND I KNEW THAT I SHOULD READ IT THIS IS WHAT THE WRITING SAID I WAS WALKING IN A CIRCLE WHEN I SPIED A

I enjoyed writing that poem so much that I wrote several more poems like it, including one in the shape of a triangle, one that winds around all over the place, and one in mirror writing. This last poem is much easier to read if you hold it up to a mirror.

Since then, I've written quite a few of these poems. For example, I've written a poem that works its way through a maze, a poem in the shape of a funnel that's about falling through that funnel, a poem that takes place inside an egg, and a *one-word poem* about an unusually clumsy owl.

Here it is: ➤

Call of the Long-winded Clumsy Owl

WHOOOOOOOOOOOOOOOOOOOOOOOOO
OOOOOOOOOOOOOOOOOOOOOOOOOOOO
OOOOOOOOOOOOOOOOOOOOOOOOOOO
OOOOOOOOOOOOOOOOOOOOOOOOOOO
OOOOOOOOOOOOOOOOOOOOOOOOOOO
OOOOOOOOOOOOOOOOOOOOOOOOOOO
OOOOOOOOOOOOOOOOOOOOOOOOOOO
OOOOOOOOOOOOOOOOOOOOOOOOOOO
OOOOOOOOOOOOOOOOOOOOOOOOOOO
OOOOOOOOOOOOOOOOOOOOOOOOOOO
OOOOOOOOOOOOOOOOOOOOOOOOOOO
OOOOOOOOOOOOOOOOOOOOOOOOOOO
OOOOOOOOOOOOOOOOOOOOOOOOOOO
OOOOOOOOOOOOOOOOOOOOOOOOOOO
OOOOOOOOOOOOOOOOOOOOOOOOOOO
OOOOOOOOOOOOOOOOOOOOOOOOOOO
OOOOOOOOOOOOOOOOOOOOOOOOOOO
OOOOOOOOOOOOOOOOOOOOOOOOOOO

(continued)

OOOOOOOOOOOOOOOOOOOOOOOOOOOOO
OOOOOOOOOOOOOOOOOOOOOOOOOOOOO
OOOOOOOOOOOOOOOOOOOOOOOOOOOOO
OOOOOOOOOOOOOOOOOOOOOOOOOOOOO
OOOOOOOOOOOOOOOOOOOOOOOOOOOOO
OOOOOOOOOOOOOOOOOOOOOOOOOOOOO
OOOOOOOOOOOOOOOOOOOOOOOOOOOOO
OOOOOOOOOOOOOOOOOOOOOOOOOOOOO
OOOOOOOOOOOOOOOOOOOOOOOOOOOOO
OOOOOOOOOOOOOOOOOOOOOOOOOOOOO
OOOOOOOOOOOOOOOOOOOOOOOOOOOOO
OOOOOOOOOOOOOOOOOOOOOOOOOOOOO
OOOOOOOOOOOOOOOOOOOOOOOOOOOOO
OOOOOOOOOOOOOOOOOOOOOOOOOOOOO
OOOOOOOOOOOOOOOOOOOOOOOOOOOOO
OOOOOOOOOOOOOOOOOOOOOOOOOOOOO
OOOOOOOOOOOOOOOOOOOOOOOOOOOOO
OOOOOOOOOOOOOOOOOOOOOOOOOOOOO
OOOOOOOOOOOOOOOOOOOOOOOOOOOOO
OOOOOOOOOOOOOOOOOOOOOOOOOOOOO
OOOOOOOOOOOOOOOOOOOOOOOOOOOOO
OOOOOOOOOOOOOOOOOOOOOOOOOOOOO
OOOOOOOOOPS!

🦎 WRITING TIP #12 🦎 🦎 🦎 🦎 🦎 🦎

This type of poem is known as a concrete poem. It's a sort of attempt to combine poetry with art, painting a picture with words. The idea is to make the poem look like what you're writing about. Most of my concrete poems rhyme, but they don't have to. In fact most often concrete poems don't rhyme. What's important about them is the shape of the poem, the typeface that's used, the sizes and shapes of the letters, the directions in which the words go, the way that the poem looks on the page, and other special effects. Sometimes the letters and words will be in pieces, upside down, backward, in white on a black background, and so on. The only limit is the poet's imagination.

Try writing your own concrete poem. Write it in the shape of a square or a seashell or a string of beads or anything else that you can think of. Remember, it doesn't have to rhyme, so don't worry about that. What's important is the feeling that you get from looking at the poem. Good luck!

Worms and Worse

When I was around eight or ten years old, I lived in an apartment house in the Bronx. My four closest friends lived in the same building. Their names were Harvey, Lumpy, Tony, and Willie. Of the four, Willie was my best friend. Willie was a fantastic kid. He was smart, he was strong, he was fast, he was good in sports, and he was very, very handsome. In other words, Willie was exactly like me.

Like a lot of best friends, we did just about everything together, and also like a lot of best friends, we were extremely competitive, and always trying to outdo each other. Willie and I often had contests: running, jumping, wrestling, shooting hoops, that sort of thing. We were just about the same size and shape, so we were very evenly matched. Sometimes he won, and sometimes I won, but it was always close. If we got mad at each other and had a real fight, neither of us won, and we both usually wound up with bloody noses and black eyes. As soon as the fight was over, we were best friends again.

Willie and I had an agreement that if either us ever did something new that we hadn't done before, the other guy had to do it too, and that meant right away, no backing down.

It didn't matter what it was. It could have been weird or stupid or silly or strange or dangerous—or incredibly gross. If I did it, Willie had to do it, and if Willie did it, I had to do it—no excuses, and right there and then on the spot.

Of course this led to some interesting situations. For example, one day the rest of us— Harvey, Lumpy, Tony, and I—were hanging around in the street, just shooting the breeze. Nothing much was going on. That's when Willie walked out of the building and happened to look down at the street. "Hey! Look at that," he said, pointing to the sidewalk. Actually, what Willie said sounded more like "Look at dat!" *Dat* is the way we all pronounced *that* back then in the Bronx. I'll tell the rest of this story in my old Bronx accent. So Harvey, Lumpy, Tony, and I all took a look at where Willie was pointing. There was a worm on the sidewalk. Well, we'd all seen worms before, and even though this one was bigger than most, not one of those little, pinkie-size worms, we didn't think about it too much one way or the other, and I said something to Willie like "Yeah, dat's a fine-lookin' woim. Waddabout it?"

Willie grinned and said, "Y'know, dat looks good!"

I did not like what I was hearing. "Waddya mean, dat looks good?" I asked.

"Dat looks dillishus," said Willie, and without another word, he bent down, picked it up, dusted it off, and ate it—just like that.

The rest of us could not believe what we were seeing. We all started screaming at him, stuff like "Oh, man! Wattsa matta wit choo?

Are you nuts? Dat's a woim! Ah, jeez! Dat's a woim! Giddada here!" Willie just looked at us, grinned again, and belched a couple of times. Willie was always a good belcher.

As soon as Willie finished swallowing that worm, a terrible thought entered my tiny mind. *Oh, no!* I thought. *Oh, no no no no no!* And then I thought some more. *Oh, yeah!* You see, I knew because of our agreement that when Willie was done doing what he just did, I had to do it too. Not only that, but I had to try to outdo him. I hunted around the neighborhood till I found an even bigger worm, and with all my friends watching, I ate it as fast as I could. I didn't enjoy eating it one bit, but I did it. I've never eaten another worm.

When I wrote my book *Rolling Harvey Down the Hill,* I included a poem about the time that Willie ate a worm. I put in as much of the experience as I could in just a few lines, including Willie's dusting off the worm, swallowing it without chewing, and belching afterward. You can write poems based on your own experiences too—even the gross ones. Think of something weird that you've done, and list everything you can remember about it: the sights, the sounds, the smells, and your feelings. Then take some of the things you've listed, and try to weave them into a poem.

Don't be afraid to exaggerate or to add or change a fact or two if you think that might improve the poem. After all, you're not a reporter telling us exactly what happened; you're a creative writer telling a funny story and trying to make it as interesting and engrossing as possible.

exaggerate: to make something bigger, better, stranger, worse, funnier than it actually is. It's a very useful technique in writing humorous poetry.

Willie Ate a Worm

Willie ate a worm today,
a squiggly, wiggly worm.
He picked it up
from the dust and dirt
and wiped it off
on his brand-new shirt.
Then slurp, slupp
he ate it up,
yes Willie ate a worm today,
a squiggly, wiggly worm.

Willie ate a worm today,
he didn't bother to chew,
and we all stared
and we all squirmed
when Willie swallowed
down that worm.
Then slupp, slurp
Willie burped,
yes Willie ate a worm today,
I think I'll eat one too.

There are worse things than worms that you might eat. Several years ago I was in a restaurant where I had lunch . . . *once*! I never went back to that restaurant. In fact I didn't even stay to finish my meal but left in a hurry. You see, suddenly right under my table there appeared some unwelcome company. It was a rat, a *big* one, and it scampered right over my feet. I jumped up, yelled a little bit, and then ran out of the restaurant.

Around that time I was walking between three and five miles a day to stay in shape. The incident in that restaurant so unsettled me that I took an extra-long walk, about nine miles. As I walked, I thought hard about that rat, and by the time the walk was done, I had a poem in my head. Instead of simply having a rat visit me at the table, I would write about actually eating a rat. I sat down on a park bench and scribbled the poem in my notebook. Of course it didn't come out perfect the first time, and I rewrote it quite a bit. The poem is called "Rat for Lunch!"

Rat for Lunch!

Rat for lunch! Rat for lunch!
Yum! Delicious! Munch munch munch!
One by one or by the bunch—
Rat, oh rat, oh rat for lunch!

Scrambled slug in salty slime
is our choice at breakfast time,
but for lunch we say to you,
nothing but a rat will do.

Rat for lunch! Rat for lunch!
Yum! Delicious! Munch munch munch!
One by one or by the bunch—
Rat, oh rat, oh rat for lunch!

For our snack each afternoon,
we chew bits of baked baboon,
curried squirrel, buttered bat,
but for lunch it must be rat.

Rat for lunch! Rat for lunch!
Yum! Delicious! Munch munch munch!
One by one or by the bunch—
Rat, oh rat, oh rat for lunch!

In the evening we may dine
on fillet of porcupine,
buzzard gizzard, lizard chops,
but for lunch a rat is tops.

(continued)

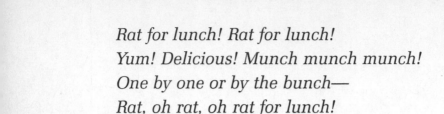

Rat for lunch! Rat for lunch!
Yum! Delicious! Munch munch munch!
One by one or by the bunch—
Rat, oh rat, oh rat for lunch!

Rat, we love you steamed or stewed,
blackened, broiled, or barbecued.
Pickled, poached, or fried in fat,
there is nothing like a rat.

Rat for lunch! Rat for lunch!
Yum! Delicious! Munch munch munch!
One by one or by the bunch—
Rat, oh rat, oh rat for lunch!

❧ WRITING TIP #14 ❧ ❧ ❧ ❧ ❧ ❧

At first I wanted to write a poem about how awful it would be to eat a rat for lunch, but then I thought about it a bit more and turned the basic idea upside down. I would write about how *wonderful* it would be to eat a rat for lunch. This is something you can do in your own writing and is called irony. When you use irony, you're describing or talking about an object or situation in a way that's the opposite of what you really mean. So when I say that I *love* eating a rat for lunch, you know that I'm just kidding. I'm being *ironic*.

Also, when you're writing a poem, you don't have to report what actually happened or even base your poem on exact facts. Take the original event and exaggerate it. You can add to it, combine it with something else that happened to you, or turn it upside down and inside out. If you do this, you'll start to see that new possibilities open up to you, that the creative process is a powerful tool. When I wrote this poem, I compared a rat with lots of other things that I thought might be gross to eat—things like scrambled slug, baked baboon, and buzzard gizzard. I simply had a good time, and you can do the same.

Think of something awful that you wouldn't enjoy eating, and write a poem about how wonderful it would be to eat that awful thing. Make it funny or silly or ridiculous or weird, and don't be afraid to experiment or exaggerate.

My Mother's Singing

Here's something else about my mother: I truly believe that she was the worst singer in the entire history of our planet. If she wasn't the worst, she was definitely in the top ten. I once watched some early episodes of *American Idol* and heard some horrible singers. My mother was worse, much worse, than any of them. Not only did my mother have an awful voice, but she was also tone-deaf. She simply couldn't carry a tune. This never discouraged her, and she loved to sing while she accompanied herself on the piano. She wasn't much of a piano player, but at least her playing was better than her singing.

Whenever my mother sang, my father, my brother, and I headed for the hills. We did our best to make some excuse to go outside, excuses like "We have to go out and count cars" and "We have to water the lawn." These excuses were obviously false and ridiculous. After all, who has to count cars? As for watering the lawn, we lived in an apartment house and didn't have one. My mother didn't pay attention to any of this and continued singing.

One morning my mother must have been especially happy. She was singing at the top of her lungs, making an unbearable racket. She sang "The Blue Danube Waltz" in a more or less minor key. The rest of us were still in our pajamas, and we hurried into our street clothes in order to get out of the apartment as fast as we could. While this was going on, someone rang our doorbell. We answered it, and there we saw a sweet little old lady who lived down the hall. She looked very sad and was carrying a big pot of chicken soup, which she handed to my father.

"Why are you giving me a pot of chicken soup?" my father asked.

The lady said, "I heard some awful noise coming from your apartment. It sounded to me like you'd had a death in the family, so I thought I'd bring some soup to help comfort you."

My father thanked the lady politely and

then explained about my mother's singing. Everyone had a good laugh over it, except my mother, who ignored all this and continued to sing. By the way, the soup was delicious.

I wanted to write a poem about my mother's singing and thought of several ways that I could do it. I could write about the rest of the family's running away when she sang. I could write about having to hold my ears. I could write about what other people thought when they heard her. There were many possibilities. Then I had a brain storm. I would write about ridiculous things that *might* happen when she sang, things that probably wouldn't and even couldn't happen but would be fun to put into a poem.

In order to do this, I did something that you can do too. I took out my notebook and made a list. This is one of my favorite writing techniques, as I've previously mentioned. I always end up with more things than I can use, but that's okay. It's much better to start with more material than you need and then eliminate some items than to start with too little material and have to scramble around for more ideas. Also, I always save the stuff that I don't use and look at it later for use in other poems.

As the list developed, I noticed that certain items worked well together and that some things could be easily made to rhyme. I've talked to lots of kids about what ridiculous things my mother's singing might inspire, and some of them have come up with better ideas than I had, even some that I would have put in the poem had I thought of them. Here are some examples: "The stars would fall off the American flag." "The planet would go out of orbit." "Your shoes would switch feet." Anyhow, here's the poem about my mother's singing, filled with some of the things that I did think of. It's called "Euphonica Jarre."

Euphonica Jarre

Euphonica Jarre has a voice that's bizarre,
but Euphonica warbles all day,
as windowpanes shatter and chefs spoil
    the batter
and mannequins moan with dismay.

Mighty ships run aground at her horrible
    sound,
pretty pictures fall out of their frames,
trees drop off their branches,
rocks start avalanches,
and flower beds burst into flames.

When she opens her mouth, even eagles
    head south,
little fish truly wish they could drown,
the buzzards all hover, as tigers take
    cover,
and rats pack their bags and leave town.

Milk turns into butter and butterflies
    mutter
and bees look for something to sting,
pigs peel off their skins, a tornado begins
when Euphonica Jarre starts to sing.

By the way, my mother saw the poem after the book was published. She read it and laughed. "I wonder where you get your ideas," she said. I didn't tell her but simply said, "Oh, they just pop into my head."

The Sounds of Words

One of my very first poems, which originally appeared in my very first book and can now be found in my book *Zoo Doings*, is called "Don't Ever Seize a Weasel by the Tail." Here it is: ⟶

Don't Ever Seize a Weasel
by the Tail

You should never squeeze a weasel
for you might displease the weasel,
and don't ever seize a weasel by the tail.

Let his tail blow in the breeze;
if you pull it, he will sneeze,
for the weasel's constitution tends to be
    a little frail.

Yes the weasel wheezes easily;
the weasel freezes easily;
the weasel's tan complexion rather suddenly
    turns pale.

So don't displease or tease a weasel,
squeeze or freeze or wheeze a weasel
and don't ever seize a weasel by the tail.

Though you might gather from the title that this poem has something to do with weasels, actually it has *nothing* to do with weasels. The poem is all about the sound of the word *weasel*.

The notion of squeezing a weasel just popped into my head one day, and I thought that it might be fun to try to fill a poem with as many *eez* words as I could. I had two rules: First, there would be at least one *eez* word in every line, and second, the words had to feel as though they belonged there. I would not put in an *eez* word if it felt forced. The lines had to flow naturally. I'll let you decide if I succeeded.

A poem doesn't always have to be *about something*. You're allowed to write a poem about pretty much nothing at all, just for the sake of writing it. To writers in general, and to poets in particular, the sounds of words are often just as important as the meanings of words. The fun and challenge are to string these words together in your own unique way.

One way of doing this is to start with a word, like *weasel, cow,* or *stew,* and then list lots of rhyming words that you think might go along with that word. Shuffle them up, try them in different combinations, and see what happens. Sometimes it works, and sometimes it doesn't.

In the case of the weasel poem, at first I

thought I would use mostly words that rhymed with *weasel,* but that didn't work out, so I decided to use those **eez** words that rhymed with the first half of *weasel,* and it worked. At least I think it did. Even if it hadn't worked, I still would have had a great time trying, and so can you.

rhyme: words or the endings of words that sound alike. *Look* and *took* rhyme, *mother* and *brother* rhyme, and *llamas* and *pajamas* also rhyme. Just because two words look as if they rhyme doesn't mean that they do. For example, *moth* does not rhyme with *both*.

You've been using rhymes all your life. Remember the nursery rhymes you used to repeat? Or how about the jump-rope rhymes and games you shouted on the playground? Rhyming gives a poem grace and charm and is an ideal way to make puns, but it's not easy to do. I always recommend that young poets shouldn't tackle rhyming until they understand other basic aspects of a poem, such as rhythm and meter and using ideas creatively and succinctly.

A Boneless Chicken

Have you ever seen a boneless chicken? No? Well, neither have I, but that didn't stop me from writing about one. Here's how it happened:

One day I was in the supermarket shopping for something to cook for supper, and I came across a package of boneless chicken breasts in the meat department. I'd seen boneless chicken breasts many times before, but that day I asked myself some questions that I'd never asked before. The questions were: What about the rest of the chicken? Was that boneless too? Could the chicken walk? Could it fly? Where did it live? What did the other chickens think about it? What kind of egg does a boneless chicken lay?

I immediately took out my notebook and jotted all this down. Then I continued shopping and let the idea percolate. I decided to write a poem about a boneless chicken from the chicken's point of view. I worked on the poem off and on for several weeks but had one problem: I couldn't figure out how to end it. This happens a lot. When it does, I go on to something else, and eventually the ending comes to me, sometimes in my sleep, sometimes while I'm working on another poem, and sometimes at the most unexpected moment. That's what happened here. I was having breakfast when that little lightbulb went on in my head. "Of course!" I said to myself. The eggs on my plate solved the ending of the poem for me. You'll have to read the poem, "Ballad of a Boneless Chicken," to see how I ended the poem. You'll also know what kind of eggs I was having when I figured it out.

Ballad of
a Boneless Chicken

I'm a basic boneless chicken,
yes, I have no bones inside,
I'm without a trace of rib cage,
yet I hold myself with pride,
other hens appear offended
by my total lack of bones,
they discuss me impolitely
in derogatory tones.

(continued)

I am absolutely boneless,
I am boneless through and through,
I have neither neck nor thighbones,
and my back is boneless too,
and I haven't got a wishbone,
not a bone within my breast,
so I rarely care to travel
from the comfort of my nest.

I have feathers fine and fluffy,
I have lovely little wings,
but I lack the superstructure
to support these splendid things.
Since a chicken finds it tricky
to parade on boneless legs,
I stick closely to the hen house,
laying little scrambled eggs.

If you'd like to try writing a nonsense poem, you don't have to think of dozens of weird things and string them together. There's a much simpler and more effective way. Start with one silly idea, and then pretend that you're a reporter, and ask the questions that reporters ask: Who? What? When? Where? How? Why? You might also ask questions like What if? and Why not? Now if you were to ask these same questions about real people, the answers would be pretty straight-forward. You'd find out the their names, where they lived, who their friends were, how they spent their time, and so on. *But* . . . if you asked those same questions about that silly thing, all the answers would be silly. That's what I did when I wrote "Ballad of a Boneless Chicken." I pretended that there really is such a thing as a boneless chicken, and I asked those same reporters' questions. All the answers were automatically silly, and I had all the material that I needed for the poem.

Another thing to think about is point of view. I chose to write the poem from a boneless chicken's point of view, because that's how it occurred to me, and it seemed to me at the time the best way to do it. However, I could have just as easily written it from another point of view, such as that of a visitor to a farm who encounters a boneless chicken, from a regular chicken's point of view, or from my own point of view. All those poems would have been quite different from one another. It's even possible that some might have turned out better than the poem I wrote. Also, I didn't have to restrict myself to a single boneless chicken. I could have written about a farm where all the chickens are boneless and perhaps where the geese and ducks and cows and pigs are boneless too. The possibilities are endless.

A Pizza the Size of the Sun

I was in a window seat on an airplane, flying cross-country on a miserable rainy day. Even though we'd broken through most of the low clouds, there was still endless rain and not a sign of the sun. I busied myself with lunch, which happened to be spaghetti. I'm a big fan of spaghetti and have written several poems about it. However, it was so gloomy outside that I was not at all in the mood to write about anything. Suddenly our plane soared through the last layer of clouds to a beautiful blue sky and a bright yellow sun. The sunlight illuminated my spaghetti, and my mood instantly changed. I wanted to write something about spaghetti and the sun, but I couldn't think of anything. Maybe I should write about the sun and some other Italian food. . . .

As soon as the notion of *other* Italian food popped into my head, I thought of pizza. After all, most pizza is round, and so is the sun. Also, if you put enough cheese on a pizza and look at it from far away, it sort of resembles the sun. I decided to write a happy poem about making a pizza that's so gigantic, it's as big as the sun. Of course this isn't really possible, especially since

the sun is many times larger than our planet,
but you're allowed to do anything you want
in a poem.

A Pizza the Size of the Sun

I'm making a pizza the size of the sun,
a pizza that's sure to weigh more than a ton,
a pizza too massive to pick up and toss,
a pizza resplendent with oceans of sauce.

I'm topping my pizza with mountains of cheese,
with acres of peppers, pimentos, and peas,
with mushrooms, tomatoes, and sausage galore,
with every last olive they had at the store.

My pizza is sure to be one of a kind,
my pizza will leave other pizzas behind,
my pizza will be a delectable treat
that all who love pizza are welcome to eat.

The oven is hot, I believe it will take
a year and a half for my pizza to bake.
I hardly can wait till my pizza is done,
my wonderful pizza the size of the sun.

You can never predict when and why an idea is going to happen. That's why besides my notebook I always carry at least two pens, in case one runs out of ink. As I said, it's not at all possible (at least in the real world) to actually make a pizza the size of the sun, but that sort of thing should never stop you from writing a poem. A poem can be about anything, and you can make it as wild or weird or impossible as you wish. After all, you're not a reporter for a newspaper, magazine, or television show, having to convey the facts about something that happened as truthfully and accurately as you can. You have the right to put anything at all into a poem. There's even a common phrase for doing this, *poetic license*. This means that you're free to write about an elephant the size of a dime, a chicken that's stronger than a hippopotamus, or a sandwich that's fifty miles long and someone who can eat that sandwich in ten minutes.

poetic license: a kind of freedom that lets writers (not only poets) change names, settings, dates, or anything else to make a particular point or create a certain feeling. Poetic license is my favorite license, and I use it all the time.

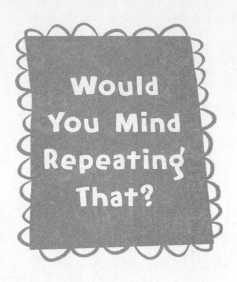

Would You Mind Repeating That?

I was at the zoo looking at a yak when I got an idea for a poem—about yaks. As far as I could tell, that yak didn't do much of anything. It just sort of stood there or walked around slowly and aimlessly. The most interesting thing about it seemed to be its long, shaggy coat. The challenge was to write a poem about a yak using just those two yak facts: the slow walk and the shaggy coat.

I worked on the poem for a while, and then the *yickity-yackity*, *yickity-yak* words popped into my head. I liked the sound of them and decided to open the poem with them and then talk about the yak's shaggy coat. The meter that I selected for the poem seemed to suggest the way that yaks walked. I had no trouble with the second and third lines but couldn't think of a last line for the first verse. Then I had a brainstorm! I would simply repeat the first line to reinforce the plodding nature of the yak. It worked.

I came up with some nonsense words for the second verse that described both the yak's shaggy coat and meandering walk. Also, I repeated the first line of that verse as the last line. The truth is that I couldn't think of anything more to say, but the poem seemed

meter: the combination of rhythms in a line of a poem. There are many forms of meters and lots of fancy ways of writing them, and even fancier ways of varying the meter to make a point or stress a particular sound or notion. This topic can get very complicated very fast. If you're a beginning poet, I suggest you use the simplest meters that you can.

In the following examples of just a few meters, I indicate unstressed syllables with a lowercase *dee*, and stressed syllables with an uppercase *DUM*.

Then I show you a sample of each of those meters with a line from one of my own poems.

dee-DUM-dee-DUM-dee-DUM-dee-DUM
My pig put on a bathing suit

DUM-dee-DUM-dee-DUM-dee-DUM
Every day, at ten pas noon,

dee-DUM-dee-DUM-dee-DUM-dee
Oh, Teddy Bear, dear Teddy,

dee-DUM-dee-dee-DUM-dee-dee-DUM-dee-dee-DUM
I wonder why Dad is so thoroughly mad,

incomplete to me; it needed something. That's when I had another brainstorm. I would simply repeat the first verse and end where I began. It's a simple technique, but it can be effective. I've always liked this poem. Here it is: ➡

The Yak

Yickity-yackity, yickity-yak,
the yak has a scriffily, scraffily back;
some yaks are brown yaks and some yaks
    are black,
yickity-yackity, yickity-yak.

Sniggildy-snaggildy, sniggildy-snag,
the yak is all covered with shiggildy-shag;
he walks with a ziggildy-zaggildy-zag,
sniggildy-snaggildy, sniggildy-snag.

Yickity-yackity, yickity-yak,
the yak has a scriffily, scraffily back;
some yaks are brown yaks and some yaks
    are black,
yickity-yackity, yickity-yak.

I also wrote a poem called "The Giggling Gaggling Gaggle of Geese," in which I used that same technique of repeating the first line of each verse as the last line of the verse. This time, however, I used the *same* line all the way through the poem. The poem has five verses, so that line, which is also the title of the poem, appears ten times in the poem. I think that it gives a gooselike, rhythmic feel to the poem that would not be there otherwise.

rhythm: the repeated beat of a poem created by the emphasis given to the syllables. In the English language the simplest rhythm is the one that goes "dee-DUM." The first syllable sounds soft, and the second sounds hard. This may be the first rhythm we ever experienced in our lives—it's the way our heartbeat sounds. Another easy rhythm is the reverse: "DUM-dee."

The Giggling Gaggling Gaggle of Geese

The giggling gaggling gaggle of geese,
they keep all the cows and the chickens
    awake,
they giggle all night giving nobody peace.
The giggling gaggling gaggle of geese.

The giggling gaggling gaggle of geese,
they chased all the ducks and the swans
    from the lake.
Oh when will the pranks and noise ever
    cease
of the giggling gaggling gaggle of geese!

The giggling gaggling gaggle of geese,
it seems there's no end to the mischief they make,
now they have stolen the sheep's woolen fleece.
The giggling gaggling gaggle of geese.

The giggling gaggling gaggle of geese,
They ate all the cake that the farmer's wife baked.
The mischievous geese are now smug and obese.
The giggling gaggling gaggle of geese.

The giggling gaggling gaggle of geese,
eating that cake was a dreadful mistake.
For when holiday comes they will make
    a fine feast.
The giggling gaggling gaggle of geese.

Repetition can be extremely effective in some poems. When you're working on a poem, ask yourself if the poem would sound better if you repeated a line or two. Be honest. Sometimes the answer is yes, and sometimes it's no. Don't repeat a line just because you're lazy and can't think of anything else. I admit that I sort of did that in the yak poem, but it worked. If it hadn't sounded right, I would have tried something else or perhaps never finished the poem.

You'll discover that most of the poems you write don't need repeated lines and might even suffer from them. You have to use your heart and your brain and your ears and your instincts to tell you when repetition is the best thing for a particular poem. I wish there were an easier way to explain this, but I can't think of one. I repeat . . . I can't think of one.

Begin
at
the End

Sometimes a pun or joke pops into my head, and I think that it might be fun to make that pun or joke the punch line at the end of a poem. The problem is getting to that punch line.

For example, I was soaking in the tub and reading an old issue of *National Geographic* magazine. There was a big article about wolves, and I started thinking about wolves and water. Then I thought of a pun about a wolf and knew that it would be a perfect (and completely unexpected) way to end a poem. Now all I had to do was figure out how to get to that punch line.

At first I thought I'd write a poem about a wolf taking a bath, so I tinkered with that idea for a little while, but I couldn't seem to make it work. Then I made a list of things about wolves that might lead to that pun . . . it still didn't work. Finally I had an inspiration. Instead of having the wolf take a bath, I would have that wolf do its laundry. The poem worked perfectly. It's called "A Wolf Is at the Laundromat."

A Wolf Is at the Laundromat

A wolf is at the Laundromat,
it's not a wary stare-wolf,
it's short and fat, it tips its hat,
unlike a scary glare-wolf.

It combs its hair, it clips its toes,
it is a fairly rare wolf,
that's only there to clean its clothes—
it is a wash-and-wear wolf.

Think of a pun, and then try to write a poem where that pun is the last line. Think of everything you can that might lead up to that pun, and make a list. I make lists for *lots* of my poems. Don't be discouraged if you can't get it to work. Not every idea leads to a poem, and sometimes I give up on one pun and try another one.

Another example using this technique is my poem "Uncle Bungle." A friend asked me, "What happens to a man who eats yeast and polish?" I said that I didn't know. My friend said, "He rises and shines."

I thought that was very clever and would

pun: a joke that arises from the way a single word can mean different things in different situations, or from playing on how words that sound the same can have different meanings. An example of the first kind is the word *seal*, which can mean a substance that sticks two things together, or the cigar-shaped mammal that lives in the ocean. I used this pun in my poem "Please Remove Seal" in *A Pizza the Size of the Sun*. An example of the second kind would be the words *toed*, meaning "having toes"; *towed*, meaning "pulled"; and *toad*, a common amphibian that resembles a frog. I used the word *towed* instead of the word *toed* to create a pun in my poem "News Brief," also in *A Pizza the Size of the Sun*.

A third kind of pun is one in which you substitute a completely unrelated word—having not the same sound but a similar sound—for the word you would expect to find. This is probably my favorite kind of pun. I think it's the most fun to invent and is possibly the sort I use most often. In my poem "The Bunny Bus," in *It's Raining Pigs & Noodles*, I substitute the word *rabbit* for *rapid*, and in my poem "A Skunk Sat in a Courtroom," in *My Dog May Be a Genius*, I substitute the word *odor* for *order*. In both cases, it's the pun that delivers the punch line and makes the poem funny. You can find many more examples of this kind of pun in my books.

make a good punch line at the end of a poem.
This turned out to be a bit easier than writing the
wolf poem, because I had extra facts—eating the
yeast and eating the polish—that I could put into
the body of the poem. Here's the poem. I'll let
you decide whether or not it's a good use of a
pun.

Uncle Bungle

Uncle Bungle, now deceased,
ate a cake of baker's yeast,
then with an odd gleam in his eye
consumed a large shoe-polish pie.

His dinner done, it's sad to say,
that Uncle Bungle passed away.
Uncle Bungle, now deceased,
still shines and rises in the east.

Poemstarts to Get You Started

If you're still having trouble getting started with a poem, then this is the chapter for you. I've written ten "poemstarts" that you can add to however you wish. It's a way to get your creative juices flowing. I supply the first two or three lines, and you get to continue the poem using your own ideas. If you want to make the poems rhyme, that's just fine, and if you don't, then that's just fine, too. Also, if you want to change or eliminate any of the words, then do it. It's okay with me. Here they are:

1. Eleven yellow elephants
   Were sitting on the floor.
   They.....................

2. I went to the market on Monday
   To purchase a couple of things.
   I...............................

3. I'm walking through a meadow
   On a sunny, sunny day.
   The ....

4. I have a friend who has a mouse
   That lives with him inside his house.
   The mouse's name is...............
   It.......................................

5. I am the captain of a ship
   That sails upon the sea.
   There is......................

6. A Blobboloon is chasing me.
It's hot upon my trail.
That Blobboloon...............

7. My favorite camel is missing.
I can't think of where it could be.
I wonder...........................

8. If I could have a dinosaur,
Which I do not have yet,
I'd...........................

9. I have a special storage box
In which I keep my monkey's socks,
My weasel's watch, my..............

10. I saw a bird this morning
That had a purple head.
It...........................

I like these poemstarts so much that I may try to write my own poems using all or at least some of them. I hope that you like them, too, and that you grab a pen or pencil and a piece of paper and start finishing these poemstarts now.

I also hope that this book has given you an idea of why I've taken such pleasure in writing poetry for more than forty years and why I find the creative process so challenging, exhilarating, and satisfying. I'd be delighted if you could feel the same way.

Here's a simple exercise that you can use to warm up: Pick an ordinary object, take a good look at it, think about it, and then write down as many things as you can about it. For example, here are ten things that I can say about the pencil on my desk.

1. It's yellow.
2. It's made of wood.
3. It has a point at one end.
4. It has a rubber eraser at the other end.
5. It can make marks on paper.
6. It's hard.
7. It doesn't bend.
8. If I tried to bend it, it would break.
9. It has printing on it.
10. It's not alive.

You can probably think of more things to say about it.

Now take something a bit more difficult, a living creature, maybe the bird outside your window, and write down as many things as you can about *that*. You could mention its size, its shape, the color of its feathers, the color of its eyes, the shape and color of its beak, the color and length of its legs, the length of its neck, the number of toes it has, the size and shape of its wings, the length of its tail feathers, and so on.

Then, if you want, take all that information, and see if you can weave some or all of it into a poem. If you don't want to write a poem about that bird, try the same exercise with something else.

Another thing you can do is ask yourself about the differences and similarities between two very different items, in this case, the bird and the pencil. Maybe they're both yellow. Maybe the pencil reminds you of the bird's legs, or maybe the pencil's point resembles the bird's beak. The whole idea is to get you thinking creatively.

Glossary

Concrete Poem   in its simplest form, a poem in which the words are arranged to look like the subject of the poem. For instance, if the poem were about circles or walking in a circle, the words would be lined up to form a circle. Sometimes the type size and the typeface are manipulated to create an image that reflects the meaning of a word or the whole poem.

Exaggerate   to make something bigger, better, stranger, worse, funnier than it actually is. It's a very useful technique in writing humorous poetry.

Haiku   a poetic form that originated in Japan. The poem is usually unrhymed and consists of seventeen syllables set in three lines. The first line contains five syllables; the second, seven syllables; and the last, five syllables. Traditionally the subject is the natural world, but many poets writing in English have found that it's a useful way of expressing insights about ordinary life.

Irony   saying something that's the opposite of the way it's supposed to be. I use a lot of irony in my poem "Rat for Lunch" when I talk about how much I enjoy eating rat. Since we all know a rat would be a horrible thing to eat, it becomes funny and silly to declare instead that it's a wonderful dish.

Meter   the combination of rhythms in a line of a poem. There are many forms of meters and lots of fancy ways of writing them, and even fancier ways of varying the meter to make a point or stress a particular sound or notion. This topic can get very complicated very fast. If you're a beginning poet, I suggest you use the simplest meters that you can.

In the following examples of just a few meters, I indicate unstressed syllables with a lowercase *dee,* and stressed syllables with an uppercase

DUM. Then I show you a sample of each of those meters with a line from one of my own poems.

dee-DUM-dee-DUM-dee-DUM-dee-DUM
My pig put on a bathing suit

DUM-dee-DUM-dee-DUM-dee-DUM
Every day, at ten past noon,

dee-DUM-dee-DUM-dee-DUM-dee
Oh, Teddy Bear, dear Teddy,

dee-DUM-dee-dee-DUM-dee-dee-DUM-dee-
    dee-DUM
I wonder why Dad is so thoroughly mad,

Poetic License a kind of freedom that lets writers (not only poets) change names, settings, dates, or anything else to make a particular point or create a certain feeling. Poetic license is my favorite license, and I use it all the time.

Point of View refers to who's doing the talking in the poem. In "Ballad of a Boneless Chicken," it's the boneless chicken who's singing the ballad. However, I could have written the poem from many other points of view, such as my own point of view (the poet as unnamed narrator), the farmer's point of view, a normal chicken's point of view, or another barnyard animal's point of view.

Pun a joke that arises from the way a single word can mean different things in different situations, or from playing on how words that sound the same can have different meanings. An example of the first kind is the word *seal*, which can mean a substance that sticks two things together, or the cigar-shaped mammal that lives in the ocean. I used this pun in my poem "Please Remove Seal" in *A Pizza the Size of the Sun*. An example of the second kind would be the words *toed*, meaning "having toes"; *towed*, meaning "pulled"; and *toad*, a common amphibian that resembles a frog. I used the word *towed* instead of the word *toed* to create a pun in my poem "News Brief," also in *A Pizza the Size of the Sun*. Here are both poems:

PLEASE REMOVE SEAL

PLEASE REMOVE SEAL BEFORE USING
  THIS PRODUCT,
the sign on the box clearly read.
I don't have a seal, but I'm taking no
  chances—
I'll toss out my walrus instead.

NEWS BRIEF

A defiant flock of pigeons
caused a minor episode
by obstructing local traffic
on a secondary road.

When the sheriff tried to move them,
they irreverently crowed,
so he radioed a tow truck
and had every pigeon towed.

A third kind of pun is one in which you substitute
a completely unrelated word—having not the
same sound but a similar sound—for the word you
would expect to find. This is probably my favorite
kind of pun. I think it's the most fun to invent and

is possibly the sort I use most often. In my poem "The Bunny Bus," in *It's Raining Pigs & Noodles*, I substitute the word *rabbit* for *rapid*, and in my poem "A Skunk Sat in a Courtroom," in *My Dog May Be a Genius*, I substitute the word *odor* for *order*. In both cases, it is the pun that delivers the punch line and makes the poem funny. You can find many more examples of this kind of pun in my books.

THE BUNNY BUS

All aboard the **Bunny Bus**,
pay your fares, and do not fuss.
You will find your ride ideal,
there's a hare behind the wheel.

Passengers, please keep your seats
as we speed along the streets.
When you're going anywhere
Rabbit Transit gets you there.

A SKUNK SAT IN A COURTROOM

A skunk sat in a courtroom.
A judge was on the bench.
He held his nose and shouted,
"What is that dreadful stench?"

"It's only me, Your Honor,"
the skunk said in retort.
"I thought I heard you calling
for odor in the court."

Rhyme   words or the endings of words that sound alike. *Look* and *took* rhyme, *mother* and *brother* rhyme, and *llamas* and *pajamas* also rhyme. Just because two words look as if they rhyme doesn't mean that they do. For example, *moth* does not rhyme with *both*.

You've been using rhymes all your life. Remember the nursery rhymes you used to repeat? Or how about the jump-rope rhymes and games you shouted on the playground? Rhyming gives a poem grace and charm and is an ideal way to make puns, but it's not easy to do. I always recommend that young poets shouldn't tackle rhyming until they understand some other basic aspects of a poem, such as rhythm and meter and using ideas creatively and succinctly.

Rhyming Dictionary   a reference book that lists more rhymes than you could possibly think of. I find it invaluable. You should be able to find one in your school or public library.

Rhythm   the repeated beat of a poem created by the emphasis given to the syllables. In the English language the simplest rhythm is the one that goes "dee-DUM." The first syllable sounds soft, and the second sounds hard. This may be the first rhythm we ever experienced in our lives—it's the way our heartbeat sounds. Another easy rhythm is the reverse: "DUM-dee."

Scansion   a fancy word for figuring out the rhythm and meter of a line of poetry.

Thesaurus   a special kind of dictionary that groups words with the same meaning. Suppose you're looking for another word for *big*. In the thesaurus you'll find that similar words are *large*, *great*, *huge*, *enormous*, and so on. This is a very useful book for writers. I always have one on my desk. You should be able to find one in your school or public library.

Voice   in poetry, the narrator of the poem. In "point of view," I said that the chicken ballad is sung by the *boneless* chicken but that there could have been a number of other narrators—for example, the farmer, normal chickens, or another animal on the farm. On a broader scale, *voice* can also refer to the unique style found in a particular writer's work. In this case, *voice* is something writers want to achieve, and often it requires a lot of writing to find it.